Dips and Skips

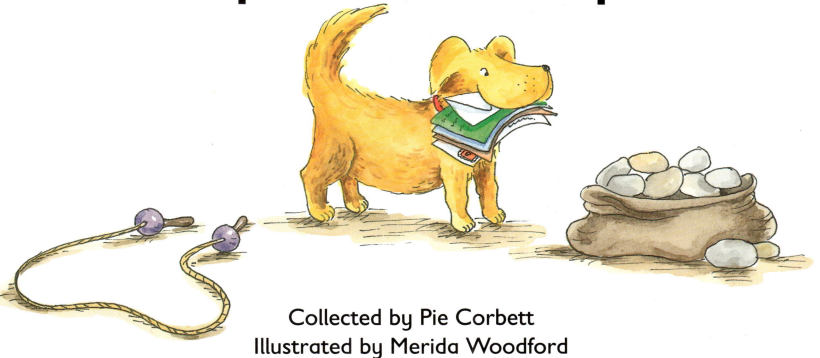

Collected by Pie Corbett
Illustrated by Merida Woodford

Collins *Educational*
An imprint of HarperCollins*Publishers*

If this book should dare to stray,
send it home without delay.

CONTENTS

DIPS

One potato...4
Did you ever?...5
Inky pinky ponky...5
Eeny meeny macker racker...6
Ipper dipper dation...7
Ibble wobble...8
Belly ache...9
Eeny meeny miny mo...9

SKIPS

I like coffee...10
Early in the morning...11
Girl Guide...12
Bumper car...13
Jelly on the plate...14
Cowboy Joe...15
Teddy bear...16

DIPS

A dip is a rhyme that you use when you need to choose someone to start a game. Dips are sometimes called 'counting out' rhymes.

One potato

One potato
two potato
three potato
four,
Five potato
six potato
seven potato
more.

Did you ever?

Did you ever see a bear
walk a tightrope in the air?
If you did it was a dream.
Out you go for saying so.

Inky pinky ponky

Inky pinky ponky
Daddy bought a donkey.
The donkey died,
Daddy cried.
Inky pinky ponky.

Eenie meenie macker racker

Eenie meenie macker racker,
rare rye domin acker,
chocker bocker lolli popper,
om pom push.

Ipper dipper dation

Ipper dipper dation,
my operation,
How many people waiting at the station?
The one who comes to number............
will surely not be it.

Ibble wobble

Ibble wobble black bobble,
ibble wobble out.
Turn the dirty dish cloth
inside out.
First you turn it inside,
then you turn it out.
Ibble wobble black bobble,
ibble wobble out.

Belly ache

I was walking round the lake
when I met a rattlesnake.
I fed him so much jelly cake
that I gave him belly ache.
One, two, three,
out goes she (or he).

Eeny meeny miny mo

Eeny meeny miny mo,
catch a baby by his toe.
If he squeals let him go.
Eeny meeny miny mo.

SKIPS

A skip is a rhyme that you sing when you are skipping. You can skip with a short rope, or turn a long rope between two.

I like coffee

I like coffee,
I like tea,
I like………..
in with me.

I don't like coffee,
I don't like tea,
I don't like………..
in with me.

Early in the morning

Early in the morning at half past eight,
you can hear the postman knocking at the gate.
Up jumps............to open up the door.
How many letters fall on the floor?
1, 2, 3, 4, 5, 6...

Girl Guide

I am a Girl Guide dressed in blue.
Here are the actions I must do.
Salute to the Captain,
bow to the Queen,
turn right round
and count sixteen.
1, 2, 3, 4, 5, 6…16.

Bumper car

Bumper car, bumper car,
number forty-eight,
whizzed round the corner,
slammed on the brakes.
The brakes didn't work,
slid down the hill,

landed in the duck pond
and then stood still.
How many fishes did you see?
1, 2, 3, 4, 5, 6...

Cowboy Joe

Cowboy Joe from Mexico.
Hands up! Stick 'em up!
Don't forget to pick 'em up!
O. U. T. spells out.

Teddy bear

Teddy bear, teddy bear
touch the ground.
Teddy bear, teddy bear
turn around.
Teddy bear, teddy bear
climb upstairs.
Teddy bear, teddy bear
say your prayers.
Teddy bear, teddy bear
turn out the light.
Teddy bear, teddy bear
say good night.
GOOD NIGHT!

See you later,
Alligator.